A year in the Country

*"I love this book. Turning the pages is
like opening a window to a country breeze!"*
—Comment of pre-publication reviewer

Publisher: Roy Reiman
Editor: Jean Van Dyke
Publications Editor: Bob Ottum
Art Director: Jim Sibilski
Production: Sally Manich

© 1988 by Reiman Publications, Inc.
5400 S. 60th St., Greendale, WI 53129

Printed in U.S.A.
International Standard Book Number:
0-89821-084-4
Library of Congress Catalog Card Number:
88-60984

Welcome to
A Year in the Country!

THERE ARE times when it seems a breath of fresh, country air is the only thing that will help you get through the day.

But, if you live in the city or suburbs, it's not always easy to get out to the country...and even if you do live in the country, the everyday concerns of life can occasionally keep you from the refreshment it offers.

Now, with *A Year in the Country* on your coffee table, you can step into the country anytime.

Page through it again and again—you'll *feel* a fresh country breeze blowing through your hair...*smell* the fragrance of wild flowers and new-mown hay...*hear* the melody of a rippling stream combining with a warbling songbird.

In your mind, you'll walk down country roads ...slide across a snow-covered landscape...lie back on the warm grass of a remote hill and admire the clouds billowing across the sky.

A Year in the Country is a mixture of fact and fancy...reflection and recreation...contemplation and celebration. Each page is filled with the revitalizing, exhilarating joys of country life— in photographs, poetry, essays and articles.

When life is hectic and crowded, noisy and stressful, come for a stay where the pace is slower...the landscapes are wide...the quiet is broken only by nature's background music... and the pressure is off. Now, turn the pages, and escape to *A Year in the Country*!

A year in the Country

52

64

65

68

80

82

95

96

The Country Awakens...

THERE'S something special about mornings in the country.

As the sun inches up to take its first peek over the horizon...as dew sprinkles your shoes, and fresh country air fills your nostrils... *these* are the moments that make every country morning special.

Come with us and listen to the quiet, as we take you on a photo tour and watch the sun rise across rural America...from the flowered valleys of California to the green mountains of Vermont...from the citrus fields of the South to the rolling wheat fields of Washington.

Our cameras have captured these early morning moments across rural America, with color pictures so vibrant you'll feel you're *there*, standing right at the edge of each place...soaking up the scents, the sounds and the scenery...and feeling the better for it.

Ready? Come to the country.

GILDING the edges of clouds (top photo), the sun lazily stretches early morning rays over fertile fields in eastern Nebraska.

FRESH LIFE greets a fresh day as a new foal stays close to mama's side, grazing dew-covered grass in southern Pennsylvania.

IN RURAL CALIFORNIA orderly ranks of grape vines wake up to a morning mist.

SERRATED SILHOUETTES of evergreens reflect morning shadows in a northern Maine lake.

DAWN'S EARLY LIGHT glints off windbent trees in quiet cove of Washington's scenic Puget Sound.

Here Comes the Sun...

FourbyFive

PRANCING thoroughbreds leave shrouded pastures and head for their early morning workouts in Kentucky's beautiful Bluegrass country.

SUN CREEPS UP on weathered split rail fence staggering along lonely back road in Blue Ridge Mountains of Virginia.

FourbyFive

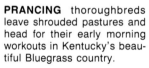

MORNING DEW captures verdant reflections along hiker's trail in northwestern Idaho.

FourbyFive

FASCINATING FENCEROW parts a field of Iowa corn as it reaches toward morning's first rays. Wonder who built this fence? And how long it's been doing its job?

HEAT'S ALREADY RISING as saguaro cactus stands sentinel in the morning quiet near Tucson.

DAWN'S GLOW seeps through early morning fog in this country panorama along the Ohio River.

CLIMBING SUN'S early rays put squash crop of a Georgia truck farm in morning spotlight. Seems sun's up, no one else is.

MOUNTAIN STREAM snakes its way down from mist-mantled foothills of a Wyoming ranch.

PROUD PINES cast long shadows on an abandoned homestead in an isolated valley in hills of Wallowa County, Oregon. *Shhh!* Listen... there, can you hear the quiet?

OMINOUS CLOUDS filter morning's first light along rugged fence corraling vast N. Dakota range land.

EAGER FISHERMEN beat the crowd and bask in beauty of Minnesota's lake country.

ASPENS VIE for share of morning sun along logging trail in Colorado Rockies. And what kind of morning is it in Vermont? Turn the page.

There's nothing like a...

Country Morning

**Got a few minutes? Then take time to share an early morning walk
down a rural road with this country mother,
as she escorts her young daughter to the school bus.**

By Judy Sizemore
Rockholds, Kentucky

"COME ON, Mommy!"

My daughter grabs her lunch box and dashes out the door. I wrap a scarf around my neck and follow her. It's still dark outside.

What a shock it is to leave the cozy warmth of our living room, the crackling fire, the cheery lights, and plunge into this world of darkness and cold. I shine the flashlight on the porch thermometer as we hurry past. Two below this morning.

"How do you stand it?" friends often ask me when I tell them how early Robin and I get up, and how far we have to walk to meet her school bus. "It must be awful."

Awful? Oh, I'll admit there is an occasional morning when the weather is bad or one of us doesn't feel well and I fire up the old truck and drive out. But most mornings are like this one. We don't want to shatter the pre-dawn silence with the roar of a motor. Our walk together down the dark road is a magical, sharing time, the best 15 minutes of the day.

"Look, Mommy, the world's all covered with diamonds," Robin exclaims gleefully, playing her flashlight across the hard sparkle of frost.

And so it is. It's a beautiful world out here. And it's all ours. We can sing without worrying if our voices are off-key. There's no one out here to hear us but the stars. Even the chickens are still sound asleep.

"Yesterday we studied all about the sun," Robin tells me. "Did you know it's our closest star?"

It's a strange thing. When she comes home in the afternoon and I ask her what she did at school, her answer invariably is "Nothing much." But now, in the crisp clarity of early morning, it all comes tumbling out: what the class learned...who sat next to her in the lunch room...who was sent into the hall for whispering.

Conversational Moments

The blackness is thinning to gray when we come to the spot where our long driveway crosses a creek. We stop on the small bridge for a moment to listen to the gurgling water.

"Why do puddles freeze before the stream does?" Robin asks as we resume our walk. Later in the day I might be too busy to answer her, but now I have time.

"I like puddles," she announces. "I like to crunch up the ice with my boots." (I still like it, too.)

"You know what I'm going to do when I grow up?" she asks, skipping ahead. "I'm going to live on a farm and raise horses and be an artist and evenings I'll give dance lessons."

"When I grow up..." So many of her sentences start with that phrase now. I look at her in the pale light. It won't be long. A dozen years and she'll be off to college...or wherever her dreams eventually take her.

That's why these walks are so precious to me. That's why I'm glad we live way down a country lane and have to walk a quarter mile to the bus stop.

She won't always be my little girl, but I'll always have the memory of these quiet, dark mornings, of our special time together.

And I hope she'll always carry the memory with her wherever she goes. I hope it will be a memory she can rest her head on when she's tired... draw strength from when she's weary ...and find peace in when she's troubled.

"There's the bus!" she cries, and we sprint the last hundred yards, making it just in time for a quick hug before the bus swallows her up and takes her away.

The sun's peeking over the horizon as I head back up the drive. I think about her on the bus, laughing and chatting with her friends. I think about my busy day ahead—the livestock to feed...the house to clean... the shed roof that needs to be repaired.

I'm ready for it now. I face my day with a smile, filled with the magic I found walking with my daughter in the darkness and cold of another quiet country morning.

Country Stream

The lovely stream
So country-free
Now skirts a hill,
Now skips a tree.
Then, leaving shade
Where willows toss
Their gray-green leaves,
It runs across

A slanting meadow
Daisy-starred,
Then lingers by
A near farmyard
Where, after seeming
Rest, once more
It turns and twists on
As before.
        —Katherine Edelman

*S*andstone ridge in Capitol Reef National Park is part of the towering, colorful cliffs and eroded landscape that fills this quarter-million acre park.
The park is named for a rock outcropping topped with white sandstone, which resembles our nation's capitol building. This photograph was taken near the Mormon farming community of Fruita, Utah.

Gene Ahrens

WINDMILLS

By Vera Schurer
St. Marys, Ohio

AS A LITTLE GIRL—growing up on a Midwest farm—the clickety-clack, whirring and turning sound of the old windmill just outside my window comforted me as I drifted off to sleep each night.

I still remember that sound—and I remember the silence when there was not enough of a breeze to turn the blades of the windmill. Then my brothers and I used hand power to pump water for the cattle. They seemed to drink twice as much water than usual on those days! After several long sessions of pumping by hand, when our arms ached with each move, what a wonderful sound it was to hear the windmill start its creaking and groaning again!

These fond childhood memories spurred me into doing a little research recently. I'd like to share with you what I learned.

Windmills have been around for almost 2,000 years, but the 19th century Americans were the ones to design a windmill that was affordable, lightweight and easy to assemble. Those windmills were needed by railroads to supply water for steam locomotives; by townspeople for running water in their new bathrooms; by Midwestern farmers for their irrigation systems; and by Western stockmen for watering cattle on their great open ranges of the land.

After the Civil War, American "tinkerers" patented *nearly 1,000* ideas for improving windmills. The first windmills had wooden sails which weathered rapidly. They were also vulnerable to prairie fires started by sparks from steam locomotives.

In 1883, Thomas O. Perry patented the first windmill wheel with metal blades. And when Aermotor, a new factory in Chicago, Illinois, began mass-producing windmills with galvanized steel blades, the American windmill industry was off and turning.

From 1880 to 1935, more than 6-1/2 million windmills were sold in the U.S. alone. By 1970, sales had declined to about 5,000 a year. Obviously, those early windmills were very durable and lasted a long time; the people who needed them already had them.

But there were two other factors which played a part in the decline: Railroads had switched to diesel engines and no longer needed water for steam locomotives. And when the Rural Electrification Administration was formed in 1936, many ranchers and farmers switched to electric pumps, which were easier to maintain and pumped even when the wind waned.

Still Rule the West

Only in the Far West have windmills remained indispensable. On the open range, windmills serve as guideposts and landmarks, as familiar as neighbors. A windmill tower has pointed the way home to many a lost cowboy.

The windmill is usually what a cowboy sees first in the distance when riding in from a cattle drive. He begins thinking about a cool drink and a hot meal while the cattle mother-up in the corrals.

For the ranch woman, the windmill is often used as a lookout tower which she can climb and look off to spot the return of her cowboy. When she sees a tide of red dust where the trails come together, she knows he's safe and it's time to put the biscuits in the oven.

The purr of the windmill is often the ranch woman's only company all day. She knows its pitch and tone, like the voice of a beloved friend, and will likely remember it until the day she dies.

Make Seasonal Sounds

Windmills speak to those who listen. Spring is seldom silent. The blades thrash and churn and chatter as the southwest wind batters the winter-worn plains. As spring storms violate the land, an old windmill turns its cheek to the anger of the storm and stands firm.

Windmills work hardest during the dry summer months. Throughout the drought, they pump day and night, sometimes kept running by gasoline engines when the wind takes a nap.

The fall wind blows fresh and clean, and since it's round-up time, all the ranch hands join in gathering up the cattle. At midday, they congregate at an agreed-upon windmill, where they're met by a ranch woman who has brought dinner in her pickup truck.

In November and December, the old windmill groans as its wheel takes in the chill wind from the north. It moves with a dull metallic twang. Snow covers the land with a quilt of white, and the rancher chops the ice on tanks and drinking tubs below the mill so his cattle can drink.

If one of these old Western windmills could spin tales, it would likely tell of blood feuds and range wars fought to the death...of hard men and brave horses...of struggling homesteaders and hungry children... of the loneliness and isolation that drove some women mad and toughened others...and remember names of those who lie beneath the shadow of its blades in unmarked graves.

But the windmill stands proud, straight and tall. It keeps its stories to itself...it just keeps turning and working in the big open country... where the wind blows free.

The Poem of a Prairie Windmill

I've spent all my lifetime
   alone on the prairie
I've watched all the seasons,
   they come and they go,
The magic of springtime,
   the hot blazing summer,
The warm, hazy autumn,
   the winter's cold snow.

I've seen the big dipper
   swing round in the heavens,
I've gazed at the Milky Way,
   far flung and high,
Been awed by the presence
   of soft friendly moonlight,
The flicker of northern lights
   low in the sky.

The bawling of cattle
   all gathered for water,
The stamping and pushing
   and milling around.
A little calf searching
   in vain for its mother,
A sullen old Hereford bull
   pawing the ground,

All this I observe
   as I stand on the prairie
And water the hungry,
   the thirsty and dry,
From morning 'til night
   and from night until morning
I'm blending my whirl
   with the coyote's cry.
               —*Joe Davis*

Fred Sieb

Spring Comes to the Country!

Tracy Borland

WHILE Summer's for sun lovers, Fall has its fans, and Winter is welcomed by snow-buffs, Spring is easily the favorite season of anyone who lives in the country!

It's a new beginning, as the soil warms and wakes...new farm animals take their first look at the world...and gardener's itch reaches the acute stage as seed catalogs are thrown aside and the first hoe *zunks* into the soil.

Come with us as we watch Spring arrive across rural America...from the black silty soils of the Midwest to the rust reds of the Southeast... from the potato fields of Maine to the orchards of Oregon.

We've recorded Spring's arrival with color pictures so vibrant you'll feel you're *there,* standing at the edge of each place as the grass greens, flowers flood the ground with color and tree buds burst.

Ready? Come to the country.

FRAMED IN FLOWERS, a horse (top photo) grazes on New York's Long Island.

GRAPEVINES at left appear to be doing early morning calisthenics in this mustard-carpeted California valley. "Reach and stretch!"

FINALLY! Springtime is slow in arriving in the state of Maine, but these fragrant blooms near Broad Cove make the season official.

Fred Sieb

The Hills Are Alive!

ABSTRACT APPLIQUE. Colorful spring growth paints patterns on this hillside in rural Oregon.

MOUNTAIN road wanders through wildflowers on ranch near Livingston, Montana, on way to distant peaks still wearing winter's coat.

FILLING a viewer's eyes and nostrils, these pristine blossoms contrast with red-as-a-blushing-firetruck buildings on New Hampshire farm.

SPRING SUN warms the dandelion-dappled field for this pair of Colorado hikers enjoying a solitary trek over a rolling, golden hillside.

Diane Gentry

Diane Gentry

Country Springs Are Special!

Fred Sieb

BLUEBONNET BLANKET spreads across Texas landscape at right, pulling a colorful cover over a rural field and warming this rural scene.

BIRCHBARK BIRDHOUSE offers an avian refuge among blossoming branches near Augusta, Georgia. Shouldn't be any problem attracting birds in a setting like this!

SPRING PASTURE occupies these Ohio horses, glad to be free from wintertime overhang barn shelter in the background. And what does it look like when daffodils trumpet the return of spring in the woods of Connecticut? Turn the page and see.

FourbyFive

COTTON CLOUDS shroud this hill and awakening trees as spring arrives in the Missouri hill country.

There's nothing like living in the country...

Especially in Spring

Share the enjoyment of this country woman as she watches winter phase out and spring ease in.

By Patricia Smith Ranzoni of Bucksport, Maine

IN THE DEEP FREEZE of Maine winters, we sometimes wonder if we should be holding on to our family homestead a few miles inland from Penobscot Bay where "Down East" begins.

Although we've insulated the house more each year and have gradually replaced most of the windows that used to ice over in November and not clear 'til March, we still have to wear extra layers against the drafts downstairs and the see-your-breath temperatures of the upstairs bedrooms.

Now that the kids have gone off to college and jobs, Ed and I sometimes ask each other and ourselves whether this old ark has served its purpose, and whether we should build or buy another place.

Then the snow banks start melting. Daylily shoots push through the thawed north yard, and we hear the roar of the rising brook through windows we've opened to the warmth of the sun and the scent of spring.

And it's then we're glad we came back to keep this farm in the family for another generation. It's as much Ed's home now and our children's as it ever was mine, though I'm an eighth and our daughter a ninth generation Hancock County woman.

Ed's working and whistling have given this valley new life and brought the sights and sounds of old country skill and survival to this New England community again. When spring comes, we know why he chose this place—with us—for his home.

We're glad when Gina's 4-H willow begins to leaf out, marking the passing of years with its height like the tall cedar planted by my young brother years ago. That cedar is allowed to stand, in honor of family, even though it blocks the loft to the stable.

We're glad when the sap rises again in the maples and, boiled down, turns into what we say is the pure taste of spring.

We're glad to capture a glimpse of a fawn frolicking on the edge of the pasture, lovely doe standing watch.

We're glad when someone yells "Ice out!" and the pond bubbles black. We know we'll soon be fishing for hornpout (freshwater catfish) to feed this year's kittens.

With the snowdrifts thinning, we can walk farther into the fields and rest with Katy and Honey, our beloved setters, by their stone markers on the ledge. From there we can look back at our place, and be glad once again that we chose to come home.

Then we wait for that first evening when the frogs sing and knowing, with the opening of trout season, the best fishin's "when the alder leaves are the size of a mouse's ear", as Grampa says. He and Gramma get the first catch, and do so with as much ceremony as the presentation of the first salmon from upriver to the White House.

That's the first thing our boys do when they come home in the spring—Gina, too—grab the poles. And it's the first thing aunts, uncles, nieces and nephews want to do when they come back.

Sometimes Ed and I join in; sometimes we just watch—basking in the satisfaction of the people and place we love—from the weathered bench that Joey made on the bank of the pond as a Mother's Day gift.

We watch and wait for the first mess of dandelion greens, then race to get our fill—boiled with salt pork and potatoes—before they break out like yellow asterisks everywhere, shouting "*Pssst!* It's Spring!"

I watch for tips of more good greens in the asparagus patch, and pace the perennial beds that Danny dug and composted where clay sod once lay among overgrown lilacs.

We've all had a hand in it, keeping this place up. The sweat of each one of us is in the soil of its fields and woods...and the soil of these fields and woods is in each of us.

"You can never go home" could not have been said by someone who loved life in the country. Euell Gibbons said it best:

I had no idea that this little corner was going to have such a different impact on me. But there the very dust is composed of the dust of my ancestors, and their bones lie under this ground.

This land formed them, and they formed me and I am tied to this country, and to its people, with bonds I cannot loosen. I had come home.

I thought I understood fully what he meant when we decided to come back, but the worn card on which I saved those thoughts so many hard winters and special springs ago has even greater meaning today. We know why we came home, and why our children come home—especially in spring.

Birds
interpret the
beauty of living
better than
anything else.

They represent
freedom,
vulnerability
and endurance.

—*M. B. Good*

Pumping iron

IT WASN'T that long ago when hand pumps, dug wells and cisterns were an indispensable source of water in rural areas and small towns.

Today's young folks will never experience the thirst-quenching capacity of a *cold* drink from a tin cup, especially after you'd "earned" it by drawing it from a deep well with a stubborn hand pump.

Did the water then really taste better...or was it because all the hand labor back in those days made us sweatier, thirstier and more appreciative of a good cold drink?

Photographer Jack Westhead, keeping his eyes and lens open, found these hand pumps scattered across rural Indiana, still standing as sentries of a simpler time when their duty was delivering a good drink instead of supporting a mailbox.

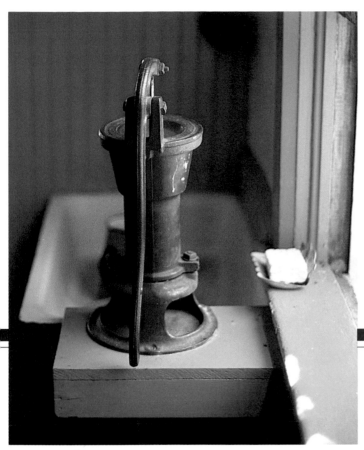

Jane Gnass

Cloud-capped mountain forms dramatic backdrop for a dairy farm near Palmer, Alaska, in the fertile Matanuska Valley. Hay, milk and produce are the main agricultural products of Alaska, where the summer sun shines for 20 hours a day during growing season, helping produce bumper crops of outstanding size. Cabbages grow to 75 pounds!

Quotes from the Country...

Good Neighbors Are Wonderful!

OUR QUESTION: "What is the most neighborly thing someone has ever done for you?" Here are the responses:

I WENT into labor with our second child 3 weeks early. My husband, Bryan, was away from the house and I had no way of getting in touch with him. A very kind and caring neighbor farm family not only made sure I got to the hospital all right, they made up a huge sign that said, "Bryan Call Home" and hung it up at an intersection they knew he'd drive through at some point in the morning.

By noon, he saw the makeshift sign and drove into their yard. The family had gone to a funeral, but they had left a note giving him details. He got to the hospital in plenty of time to help me welcome our new daughter into the world. Now *that's* what I call a good neighbor! —*Annette Krinke, Scranton, North Dakota*

MY JOB kept me from knowing many of my neighbors in the small Kentucky town where I lived. It also kept me too busy to keep our yard up. One day, driving past an attractive estate I'd always admired, I saw a handyman trimming bushes. I stopped and asked if he'd be willing to do some yard work at my place.

He agreed, and came to my house a short time later. My wife gave him specific instructions. He pruned and trimmed and did a fine job.

When he finished, I offered to pay him, but he refused to accept any money. I insisted, pointing out that he got paid at the place where I'd met him, so why not here? That's when he corrected me. "No, I don't get paid there, either. I own the place. Doing the yard work is my hobby." When I

stammered an apology and my thanks, he told me he was just trying to be a good neighbor! —*George Carroll, Winfield, Kansas*

I WAS on my way to choir practice when I had a flat tire. My neighbor's house was just ahead, so I decided to make it to the light of his yard light before changing the tire.

Jim came out of his house as I was getting the jack from the trunk. When he found out I was on my way to choir practice, he told me to take his car and go on.

Reluctantly, I did. When I got back after practice, my car was ready to go. And we don't even attend the same church! —*Clinton Tenniswood, Melvin, Michigan*

LOSING everything you own in a fire can be a frightening experience, but it also can show you the quality of your neighbors. Ours near Pollock, Louisiana donated a place for us to live until we could rebuild, donated clothes, food, furniture and even cash, although most of them were struggling to make ends meet.

The neighbors also helped rebuild our home, helping with carpentry, electrical work and plumbing after they had worked all day at their jobs. Good neighbors are a real blessing! —*Darlene Dufour, Pineville, Louisiana*

LAST APRIL my husband died suddenly and unexpectedly. The next morning, as the word spread through our neighborhood, the phone and the doorbell didn't stop ringing as people called, came and went.

Our little dog, Ernie, confused by the commotion, alternately hid under the furniture and got underfoot. He missed his master and his morning walk. The doorbell rang again and this time it was our 8-year-old neighbor, Tina. She simply said, "I came to take Ernie for his walk."

With all the thoughtful things my neighbors did at that time—bringing food, flowers, cards, letters, memorials—the thing I'll always remember most is the thoughtfulness of Tina, who did what she could by taking Ernie for a walk. —*Lois Borden, Grants Pass, Oregon*

NEARLY 20 years ago, my husband left me with four children—the youngest only 1 month old—and no financial support. On a cold March day, I answered a knock at the door. A representative from the gas company was standing there with a wrench in his hand. He told me he had come to turn off the gas.

Then he looked at me, holding the baby, surrounded by my three curious daughters. He lowered his head, stepped back away from the door and said, "Ma'am, if your heat gets turned off, someone else is going to have to do it." Then he turned and left.

The gas company later extended us the courtesy of credit to get through the cold winter months, and the thought of their generosity still warms me today. Many folks don't usually think of a utility company as being a neighbor, but if you separate the workers from the corporation, you have a good neighbor. —*Pauline Hostetler, Palmyra, Pennsylvania*

WHEN we moved from the city, I didn't know much about country neighborliness, but I learned fast!

Four months pregnant and surrounded by boxes, I was too busy to think about Halloween. It was a pleasant surprise when our new neighbor offered to take my twin 7-year-old daughters and 4-year-old daughter trick-or-treating!

That was 9 years ago. Since then, I've seen time and again that country neighbors are there when you need them.
—*Eileen Runyon, Brockport, Pennsylvania*

36

That flower…
So simple
Tall and elegant
Among all riches
It cost so little.
Yet what value…
It possesses the aroma of
The most sensuous perfume
The color of top fashions
The touch of the softest velvet
The grace of a princess
And the kiss of sunshine.

—*Teri Deblieck*

Bill Gleasner/Stock Market

Suddenly It's Summer!

Guy Graybill

SUMMER in the country doesn't ease in...it's a "happening". You get up one morning, step outside, take a deep breath and it's *arrived*.

A country summer is a sensory season, filled with pungent smells, soft sounds, savory tastes, radiant sights and soothing sensations.

It's a ripe and juicy time of year ...fresh foods overflow the garden, roadside markets and pickup trucks. You can even *taste* summer, from tart lemonade to the sweetness of a just-picked berry, from a squirtingly ripe tomato to the melting pink of a watermelon heart.

Summer is by turn luxuriant, lethargic and lush. There's room in the season for wild adventure and hammock sitting...for "hurry before it rains" and solitude...for barefoot freedom and a natural tan.

Our photographers captured summer's arrival across the country. Ready for a tour? Turn the page.

PLACID POND'S calm (top photo) is broken only by the plop of line as young fishermen try their luck in northern Georgia.

SNOW-CAPPED even in the summer, Mt. Rainier provides a picturesque background for colorful profusion of summer blooms.

RUBY RED juice of these succulent wild berries will be ample reward for pickers. "That's one in the pail, two in the mouth!"

Deanna Larson

FourbyFive

BROAD BRIMMED STRAW HAT shelters this sun-basked gardener bent to her mission—even weeding is a pleasure on this balmy day in Illinois.

SUNLIT SWINGING. The barefoot freedom of an endless summer stretches blissfully ahead for this lucky youngster bathed in sun's gold glow.

FERNS UNFURL on floor of this Idaho forest. These primeval woods have the same timeless look and quiet air that they've had for eons.

SHELTERED VALLEY basks in summer's sun. This little-traveled backroad runs through unglaciated southwest corner of Wisconsin.

SERENE SILENCE of daybreak surrounds these two sailors casting off from a North Carolina pier. Who's captain, and who's crew?

ANTICIPATION. Action is frozen a moment before swimmer plunges into welcome cold of refreshing swimming hole in upstate New York.

SUMMER CELEBRATION. Reunions (such as the July 4th picnic in Maine at far right) are synonymous with summer, as families gather to share favorite dishes and catch up on all the family news.

Ken Dequaine

Doris Barker

Simon Wolfe/Stock Market

Barbara Feigles

COTTON CANDY CLOUDS billow over horizon as bass fishermen go for the big ones in Oklahoma lake.

BRIGHT MORNING SUN lights crayon-colored setting where this young "truck farmer" offers some of Mom and Dad's home-grown produce from Ohio garden. Both he and his products are hard to resist.

SUMMER BOUNTY. Produce stand pictured at right offers "early pickings" at New Jersey farm market.

DAY LILIES volunteer to do their part for rural beautification across the countryside. For photo evidence of the role they play in a super setting along a curving Wisconsin backroad, turn the page and go ah-h-h-h!

42

RUSHING WATER tumbles through rocks and rills in a West Virginia stream, splashing mossy bank.

SAMPLING TASTE OF SUMMER. Nothing smacks of summer like a hot dog eaten outdoors...candy apples in bright red rows...and a refreshingly sweet ice cream cone that makes you hurry so you can stay a lick ahead of the melting.

43

Gift of a Day

Saturdays are special for this Tennessee grandmother when she shares the day with one of her grandchildren.

By Dee Myhan
Lawrenceburg, Tennessee

ANTICIPATION of the day sparkles in Jason's eyes. His headlong rush into my arms confirms his joy at being alive on this Saturday in June: "Gramma, I've come to play with you!"

We wave goodbye to his parents with the happy awareness that this is *our* day. The sunshine melts over the morning in a blessing of high blue sky and soft summer breeze as we head out for our country walk.

No prosaic, traditional cereal-eggs-bacon-fruit breakfast for this 5-year-old today. No, sir. This morning it is a do-it-yourself peanut butter and grape jelly sandwich eaten on the go between inspections of spider webs, closeups of mole tracks and a silent observation of blue bird eggs.

Our shoes are soaked with dew—the perfect excuse to go barefoot as Jason prepares his armada to sail on a sea of sand and water. A trip to the barn and the wheelbarrow is loaded with wreckers, dump trucks, bull-dozers and jeeps. The hose is brought to the edge of the sand and turned on. Soon shovels and hands have made miniature lakes, rivers and islands. Vehicles bog down and spin out as the driver dictates.

The sun stands high overhead and the morning evaporates in endless questions with deep philosophical undertones. "Gramma, are you old? Will you die? Why doesn't Granddad have hair on his head?"

We sing old nursery rhymes, learn new ones, fathom the mystery of his father being my little boy, and try to capture an uncooperative frog that insists on hopping into the herb garden. Peppermint, lemon and sage leaves are separated into their special smells and all become a part of Jason. Lunch is a trade-off. He eats a carrot, an apple and a piece of cheese as I take him to the creek. This is the ultimate Shangri-La for a little boy. What

is normally a 10-minute stroll for me extends into an hour-long expedition with him. First, there's the dogwood tree to climb. From a perch high in the rigging, a captain surveys his deck, awash with field daisies.

The vineyard is inspected for the first signs of grapes. Next, we stop by the garden for a visit with the scare-crow and speculation on when the corn will have ears on it. On the downhill path through the woods there are ferns to step over very care-fully; mushrooms and toadstools to talk about; May apple skirts to tip in search of the shy, lonely flower.

Suddenly all other thoughts leave Jason's mind—he hears the creek and rushes pellmell toward the sound. The cascading water gurgles over little rills and spills through natural rock gates where minnows romp in un-disciplined freedom.

Jason wades right in. He doesn't even think about the icy temperature of the water. There are rocks to turn over and, if he is lucky, a crawfish will hurriedly abandon his homestead. A pencil-thin snake with its head on lookout wiggles his way across a rif-fle. Jason misses none of this. His chatter has stopped. He is totally ab-sorbed in a world only 5 years old.

As shadows climb up and the air turns cooler, I call, "Jase, we must go." He looks at me from the outer limits of his imagination and pleads for just one more minute.

Finally we climb slowly up the hill path, hand in hand. When Grand-daddy comes home a whole new area of activity is open to Jason. He abandons Gram-ma without a backward glance. Sit-ting on Granddaddy's lap on the trac-tor, he begins learning the basics of

guiding a wheeled vehicle on a pre-scribed path, around and around the roadway, with Gramma a cheering section of one.

At dinner, there's no snacking. Men *eat.* Granddaddy eats steak, salad and potatoes. Jason eats steak, salad and potatoes. Muscles are brought out and admired. Arm wrestling is proposed, but Gramma insists that etiquette wins hands down at table.

Then it's the time of the firefly. Jason, armed with a bug catcher, heads out to capture his personal miniature lanterns.

A glass of milk and a spoonful of peanut butter fortifies Jason for the night. Story time stretches over Hansel and Gretel, Jack and the Beanstalk and Pinocchio. At last, we are lying down. The fireflies on the bedside table keep blinking, hypno-tizing me into near sleep.

But Jason's not ready to end the day. Left-over energy runs through him like an electrical current and he nearly glows in the dark.

"Gramma, tell me a story."

"Jason, I've read you three stories. Now it's time to say good night and go to sleep."

"Just one quick story, please."

"Oh, all right. Which one do you want to hear?"

"Three Little Pigs."

I tell a condensed version in less than a minute. He sighs and says, "Boy, that was a quick one! Good night, Gramma. I love you."

On such a day, it's impossible to say who had the most fun. For a 50-year-old grandmother, the world became new again, for there is some-thing special even in watching an ant move a cracker crumb if you see it through the eyes of a 5-year-old. For Jason, to have the complete, undi-vided and loving attention of an adult for one whole day is a feeling of un-limited power and fulfillment as a person of some importance.

There will be many more of these days, with many different adventures. But for now, we'll both savor this Saturday in June, when Jason came to play with me!

Doris Barker

Sunbaked Country Kids

Paul Miller

I love the sunbaked country kids
Running wildly through July
They play with such abandon
Beneath the bluest sky

I hear their laughter's music
Floating freely through the air
Long chains of tangled dandelions
Placed round their necks with care

With puppy dogs and corn on cob
Picnics in the sun
Water fights and mud slides
Summer days can be such fun

I love the sunbaked country kids
Every day of every year
But I enjoy their wild antics
Most of all when summer's here!

TERI DEBLIECK

Teri Deblieck

Gene Ahrens

Golden waves of wheat stretch on, acre after acre, set off by misty purple contours of already harvested and plowed fields. Palouse Valley, in the southeast corner of Washington state, with its gently rolling hills and deep, fertile, moisture-holding soils, is where grain farmers grow a large portion of the state's wheat— its most valuable crop.

There's nothing quite as fragrant
As the scent of new-mown hay,
Wafted on the summer breeze,
Cured by sunshine where it lays.
I've smelled jasmine, rose and violet,
And I love their sweet bouquet,
But to my way of thinking
They can't compare with new-mown hay.

It's the smell of sun and country,
Bees buzzing in the flowers,
A barefoot boy a-fishing,
Whiling away the happy hours.
I get so very homesick,
When I smell that new-mown hay,
For it brings back childhood memories
Of that far-off yesterday.

What Is 'Country'?

By Teri DeBlieck, Gerlaw, Illinois

SUDDENLY, country is "in" with home decorators, clothes designers and travelers seeking out a country inn. So some may ask, just what is "country"? Since I live there, I think I'm qualified to answer.

Country is a feeling that's warm and welcoming. Its main ingredients are love and laughter.

Country can be old or new, light and lacy, or rough and rustic. It can be whimsical, too, like patching an old worn pillow with multicolored thread and tiny hearts.

Country is being comfortable and content whether it's "stylish" or not...like setting boots by the register to keep feet warm at chore time ...or storing the evening's bath towels in the oven still warm from baking.

Country is finding the first ripe strawberry and splitting it six ways. It's children swinging from an old rope when 50 feet away is a brand new swing set.

Country is an assault on the senses ...the smell of a fresh-baked pie cooling on the sill...jelly simmering on the stove...newly tilled earth after a summer shower mixed with the smell of sheep, cows, horses and chickens.

Country is cherishing that massive old table in desperate need of refinishing...because it was Mom's. And Grandma's before her.

Country is taking a walk on a perfect morning when you should be washing the kitchen windows...looking for a rainbow when you should catch up on the bookkeeping...turning the jump rope for the kids when work is waiting.

Country is a puppy dragging off your sneakers for the hundredth time ...a little girl's squeals as she's being chased by a bib-overalled menace carrying a fat toad...it's bringing a warm cake to a new neighbor.

Country is to be appreciated.

Marilyn S. Rogers

Julie Habel

Country Road, Take Me Home...

Lester Tinker

IF YOU haven't done it for a while, it's time you do it...turn off the main highway—away from the toll-ways and cloverleafs—and head down a tranquil country road.

Turn off the air conditioner and roll down the car windows. Let in the breeze, the sights and the sounds that soothe, surprise and revitalize. The journey is important, the destination isn't.

Get even closer. Pull off to the side of the road, with the right wheels sinking into the grassy shoulder, then get out and walk.

Forget your schedule for a few minutes. You owe yourself this kind of country respite. Listen to the gravel crunching beneath your shoes...the leaves rattling in the trees...the wildlife calling and skitting here and there.

What? You can't get away just now? Then do the next best thing. Saunter along as our photographers take you on a colorful tour of country backroads. C'mon...join us.

GAGGLE OF GEESE, backlighted by morning sun, strings across a county road in rural Iowa, forming a reception committee for school bus approaching on morning route.

WENDING ITS WAY through spruce trees in southwestern Colorado, a logging road clings to the mountainside, segmenting scenery.

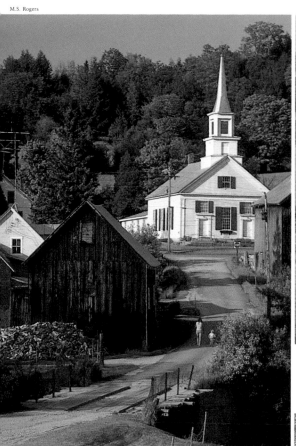

VERMONT VISTAS. Waits River's main street (left) is traveled by a pedestrian pair; below, the graceful sweep of this rural road is punctuated by birch tree exclamation points.

DIPPING ACROSS gently rolling hillsides, country road near Ellsworth, Wisconsin undulates past well-kept farms, ripening crops.

M.D. Bavati

Country Roads...

ZIG-ZAG HEMSTITCH of rail fence borders this grassy country lane in West Virginia. Trees add their leafy ruffles...it's country decor at its best!

BACKROADS BECKON, tantalizing tourists and locals who travel the three New England roads shown at right. Who knows what you'll find around that black-topped curve near Plainfield, Vermont...or where these young bikers are headed in the morning mist ...or what adventures are ahead for those three daffodil-slickered strollers headed through a tunnel of trees?

PASSAGE TO THE PAST, this covered bridge evokes images of horse-drawn days. Just imagine hoofbeats echoing from the bridge, one of only 54 covered bridges left in Oregon.

C.L. Handy

George Robinson

COW CROSSING. These leisurely ladies stroll across a country road in New Hampshire. They must be pretty polite Holsteins, if that birch-log fence is enough to keep them in!

Country Roads...

Sally A. Beyer

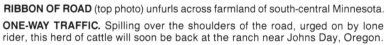

Vernon Selde

RIBBON OF ROAD (top photo) unfurls across farmland of south-central Minnesota.

ONE-WAY TRAFFIC. Spilling over the shoulders of the road, urged on by lone rider, this herd of cattle will soon be back at the ranch near Johns Day, Oregon.

Martha Moore

CAMARADERIE. Comfortable companions mosey down a gravel road, ready to get an early start on morning chores on their Vermont farm.

INTREPID EXPLORER plans his next move as he hangs on gate in Michigan. He'll be gallivanting all over the countryside in just a minute...making new discoveries...building memories he'll surely savor for years to come.

HEADIN' INTO THE SUNSET, this wrangler rides modern day horsepower down a country road to mountainous horizon in Washington State.

George Robinson

Les Kelly

PASTORAL PEACE surrounds Amish boy riding his bicycle past contented cows in Holmes County, Ohio. And when you turn the page, you'll find yourself trekking down a Mississippi road, overhung by trees at the lush peak of their season.

John Pratt

Quotes from the Country...

Readers Tell Why They Like Country Life

OUR QUESTION: "For you, what is the most satisfying thing about living in the country?" Here are the responses:

SCIENTISTS say that certain smells bring back the memory of our earliest years. I feel the same is true of sounds—and sounds are what I like best about living in the country.

When I wake in the early morning hours to the melodious tune of the meadowlarks, the song enlivens my heart for the day ahead. And when I go to bed at night, the whisper-soft cooing of the doves plants peace deep within my soul.

These were my favorite sounds when I was a little girl growing up in an orange orchard—they were accompaniment to carefree days and restful nights. They're still my favorite sounds today. *—Marcia Moffitt, Cornville, Arizona*

IN MY MIND, roaming through our fields of hundreds of wildflowers has to be the most pleasurable experience in country living. Graceful white daisies, their yellow button eyes turned to the blue sky...shy purple and white violets cowering close to the ground... buttercups offering their gold...Queen Anne's lace, so commonplace yet dainty and intricate...bluebells winking as we pass...butter and eggs so richly yellow and orange...black-eyed susans playing in the sunlight...the purple clover offering its delicacies to the bees.

They're all here for us to enjoy, as well as their attendants—the lovely butterflies, comical grasshoppers, feathery moths and swooping dragonflies. With such beauty all around, country life is just great! *—Betty Hapta Woodbridge, New Jersey*

I HAVE LIVED on a farm for 26 years. My husband and I have worked the land, and cared for it, and it in turn has given much to us. The satisfactions of country life for me include the freedom to really be yourself, and to be in tune with nature...the fulfillment of watching the seeds you've planted grow into a fruitful crop... the joy of seeing your children learn from the land...the contentment of watching a beautiful sunset at the end of a long day, or a rainbow after a storm.

The most satisfying facet of country life is togetherness, as my husband and I walk over the land, happy we share our love of each other, of nature, of our farm, and of life in the country. *—Carolyn Schneider, Portage, Ohio*

WHEN I step outside on a warm summer morning I can feel the sun streaming through the early morning mist. I can see chipmunks and squirrels skittering around, the bees busy in the flowerbed and field, the birds chirping and flying about. I can smell the damp earth, bringing the promise of growth.

I walk along a little patch and pick berries from the vine. All is quiet, except for nature's sounds, and I am in the midst of it—free, alive and in harmony with God's creation. *—Mary Jane Gast, Randallstown, Maryland*

WHAT'S MOST satisfying? A *deep breath!* That is not necessarily because the air is clearer. I'm talking about the kind of deep breath you take when you get the last bale of hay in the barn...the deep breath you take when you straighten your stiff back after weeding the green beans...or that deep breath that even shudders your heart when a new foal runs to greet you in the morning dew.

It's the kind of deep breath that has roots, deep roots into the land God has shared with you to build a heritage. Living in the country gives one lots of opportunities to stand tall, glance skyward, and take a deep breath. *—Polly Jo Stryker, Dighton, Massachusetts*

PEACE has to be the most satisfying aspect of country life for me. Not silence, for after all the country is not without sound...sounds such as the bubbling giggles of a running creek, the rhythmic pecking of a busy woodpecker, the whoosh of the breeze pushing its way through the tree leaves.

But the peace of the country makes it a place where you can feel stress and tension being pulled from you... a place where nature's undisturbed condition can be enjoyed and appreciated to the fullest.

As I tell people—if you want silence, close yourself in a closet. If you want peace, go to the country! *—Gwen Simmons, Centerville, Iowa*

SEASONAL changes are what make country living so satisfying. We savor breathtakingly beautiful spring mornings, with their background music of phoebes nesting, distant cows mooing and our miniature horses whinnying as they nibble sparse new grass.

We relish the absolute peacefulness of summer afternoons, sipping lemonade by our little lake.

We revel in brisk autumn's glorious trees, dressed in yellow, orange, red and purple, until fall fades into winter's restfulness. *—Mr. and Mrs. Louis Wintermeyer, Kerhonkson, New York*

Country Sunset

Soft opalescent pinks and blue
of fluid sunset sky
show abalone pearl-tipped clouds,
sea-shells—hung up to dry.

—Marianne McFarland McNeil
Amarillo, Texas

Sunflower's golden heads nod in a field in Wisconsin's Door County—the peninsula that forms the "thumb" of the state's mitten shape. Quaint fishing villages, artists' shops, music festivals, outdoor theaters, cherry orchards, Swedish delicacies and fish boils—as well as picturesque farms such as this—make it a prime vacation haven.

A Place Of
Wonder

By Jan Jones
Fair Haven, Vermont

RACHEL CARSON said it best: "If I had influence with the good fairy who is supposed to preside over the christening of all children, I should ask that her gift to each child in the world be a sense of wonder so indestructible that it would last throughout life..."

Few of us have personal friendships with the fairies these days. Instead, we must seek out a place for our children...a place where the rhythms and textures of life weave their own kinds of spells...where the images, music and scents of the earth are still pure enough to haunt the imagination.

I know we're in the right place when our 3-year-old says in hushed tones, "Isn't that bird beautiful? It sounds like church bells!" It's a wood

"OUR BABIES LISTEN TO FOREST LULLABIES..."

thrush, singing in the early evening, and suddenly the forest becomes a temple to me, too.

Time seems different under the trees. We slow down. With our little ones, we begin to see the things that usually pass unnoticed—such as long, stretchy rays of late afternoon illuminating a patch of lichens, a lustrous yellow birch, a dappled forest floor that changes moment by moment, a bold orange eft, brilliant mushrooms, and a nest of empty grouse eggs.

Adventuring we go, over logs and through tall ferns. We never know

what treasure we might find, but always know that there *will* be a treasure. Sometimes breathtaking—cecropia moths in the mist. Sometimes dramatic and disturbing—a snake eating a toad. Sometimes startling—a leaping frog or a beaver tail smacking the pond.

We emerge from the trees at the pond's edge, in the meadow of jewel-like bugs and wildflowers, of whispers and hums and webs that quiver. Here, the sky speaks to us the most.

The sky, so intensely blue against the forest that chickory and bugloss and fragments of robin's egg are pale in comparison. The sky, holding clouds that look like "mandarin oranges" one day, and "huge, fierce allosauruses" the next.

When darkness falls, the twinkle of meadow fireflies echoes the greater show above. That's when we lie on our backs to watch and discuss the stars. And on special occasions when the aurora borealis floats veils of color across the back pasture, it almost urges us to make up dances to imitate the shifting light.

We don't need to hum or sing lullabies to our babies out here in our country home—our babies listen to swamp and forest lullabies...to tree frog choruses and sweet trills of

"TIME SEEMS DIFFERENT UNDER THE TREES."

toads...to wind in white pines...to rain dripping from canopy to understory...to night songs of owls and coyotes...and to the soft sound of cows chewing in the lot by the barn.

This gift of wonder passes from parent to child to parent to child, in a form of recycling that will remain whole and indestructible, if the foundations are laid in a magical place.

Vermont—where we live—is such a place. Perhaps there is a fey element after all, a fairy ring surrounding us as we step outside our country home together and say *"ahh..."*.

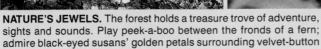

NATURE'S JEWELS. The forest holds a treasure trove of adventure, sights and sounds. Play peek-a-boo between the fronds of a fern; admire black-eyed susans' golden petals surrounding velvet-button centers; sit on a log to examine nature's miracles; admire an emerald-green frog in a leafy setting; gather yellow-dipped daisies and chain them together to create a necklace as prized as any string of pearls.

ONE HAS ONLY TO SEE

*The Natural Beauty of
Country Life Is Outstanding…
Yet Sometimes,
Unfortunately, Overlooked.*

Country

By Judy Hubers
Pantego, North Carolina

Everyone who lives in the country shares a good deal of the same type of beauty in their surroundings. It's unfortunate that not everyone has learned to *see* that beauty.

Our family learned to see and appreciate it by spending time outside …not just time doing our work and chores, but time spent in walking, listening and feeling…in stopping, touching and smelling. Marvelous discoveries are made this way.

It was through photography that our teenage sons and I have come to really appreciate the often-overlooked wonders surrounding us. Through the camera lens we now focus in on the beauty, get a close-up view and save it for further enjoyment and sharing.

The photograph here and those on the following pages show some of the natural beauty we enjoy; they reflect our appreciation of the world around us. One of the greatest pleasures for my husband and me has been in seeing our children learn to appreciate the small things of life, created for us all to enjoy.

When we hear, "Mom, come outside! there's this bird…" or, "Mom

ONE
HAS ONLY
TO SEE

Caterpillar hunting is done mostly by our 10-year-old daughter, Stacie. She especially enjoys looking for the caterpillars of the spicebush swallowtail butterflies.

In our area, these butterflies lay their eggs on sassafras trees, and when a little caterpillar hatches, we watch them eat the sassafras leaves. They also spread silk over a leaf and pull the leaf edges together, forming a haven from predators.

According to Stacie, looking for rolled-up leaves and opening them to see if the caterpillar is still inside is better than an Easter egg hunt!

The chrysalis can be just as fascinating as the caterpillar. We've observed that each species forms a different kind of chitin shell, with different shapes, colorings and markings. Most resemble twigs, dry leaves or even bird droppings to foil the enemy.

But closer inspection reveals intricate designs. The question mark butterfly chrysalis has a cat-like head with round ears and metallic-gold eyes and a laced-bodice pattern at the end attached to the twig end.

Sometimes I try to figure out why a chrysalis is marked the way it is—I think it's just because God enjoyed making them that way!

have you seen that *sunrise*?'' or ''Hey, Dad, the swans are coming in!'' we always drop whatever we're doing and take a moment to share the wonder with our children.

We're surrounded by wildlife at our country place, but nature's beauty isn't only in birds, animals and butterflies. It's in the sunrise...the sunset...the pattern of spring buds against the sky...the sunlight glowing through colored leaves and petals ...in dewdrops on spider webs and fog in the woods. It's rain-blackened tree bark and reflections in puddles. It's masses and ferns and green-blue irridescent beetles. It's snow and frost and ice and summer's clouds and rainbows.

It's endless. And it's always there. One has only to *see*.

The pleasure of observing the caterpillars and chrysalises is surpassed only by the excitement of the emergence of colorful creatures such as this tiger swallowtail.

Our children have noted that at first a butterfly's or moth's wings are shriveled, the body engorged with fluid. Within minutes, the fluid is pumped out of the body into the veins of the wings, expanding them into broad, patterned sheaths.

I build blinds so our family can all watch birds in the shrubbery. When I investigated a female cardinal carrying straw to a catbrier tangle, I found a nearly completed nest.

I photographed the nest daily after the eggs hatched, and continued until the young birds fledged. The most exciting of the 8 days the young were in the nest was this rainy day when I slipped into my blind to find the female cardinal sitting on the nest, soaking wet, with three snuggly warm babies deep in the nest.

After 10-15 minutes, I heard the male call as he approached the nest. The female brightened as the male lighted near the nest and gave her half his catch. I caught that intimate moment with my lens.

Together, they stood on the side of the nest and fed the babies. Then the male flew off to find more food, while the female settled back down on the nest to brood her babies.

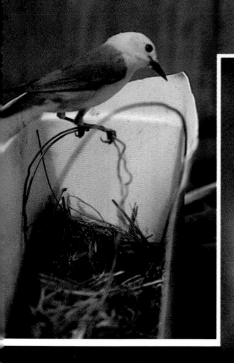

This young screech owl stopped me in my tracks the first time I found a grayish-white, downy ball of fluff sitting on the workbench in our shop! We put it back into the nest, but found it on the bench 2 days later. It fell twice more before I decided to leave it alone.

The little owl's mother continued to feed it at night, and it grew and moved around. We never knew where we'd find it in the morning, but it spent so much time in the parts bins our hired men began to call it "Parts".

When his wings worked so well he could fly up to a fan belt hanging from a rafter (where he perched and slept for the day), we thought he was making great progress. But eventually the morning came when "Parts" wasn't in the shop anymore. We all missed him after that.

We don't always have to head to the bushes and the shrubbery to observe birds—sometimes they come into our shop and set up housekeeping! This little yellow and black prothonotary warbler is a regular tenant, sometimes nesting in the parts bin—and once in a cut-off antifreeze can!

Capturing on film certain small pieces and special moments of nature—such as the web-draped morning glories and frog with water lily—lets us preserve and share the beauty of our country place.

Our teen-aged sons came home very excited one day, after watching a family of young foxes play around some of our machinery while they were sitting on it! Apparently, the foxes were used to machinery, and since the tractors had cabs, they didn't realize humans were present. The kits climbed all around, tumbled, tussled and explored for a very long time, and our sons were fascinated by every minute of it.

Frank Houck

Beauty Abounds as Autumn Leaves

Grant Heilman

GET SET for rural America's seasonal spectacular! Nature's gearing up for its annual theatrical performance, changing the set from energetic summer to mellow autumn.

Your "ticket" costs no more than a trip to the countryside. There you can enjoy the show of natural wonders...some as gaudy as a three-ring circus...others as subtle as a museum diorama.

Now's the time to store visual treats to your memory...such as a pumpkin-hued harvest moon caught in the branches of a tree shedding summer...a vermilion leaf floating on a placid pool...a panoramic view of a valley in harlequin hues.

Memories such as these will brighten the winter days ahead.

Our alert photographers have captured fall's flamboyance at its colorful peak. So join our tour group as we "ooh" and "ahh" across the country. C'mon...we have to hurry...before autumn leaves.

MULTI-HUED trees add a splashy explosion of color to the background of Saranac River at Clayburgh, New York.

LICHEN-COATED rock outcropping, with its crimson slash of maples and sumac, angles across sapphire lake in Yukon Territory near edge of Alaska.

RICH, RUSSET leaves veined in green spread their lobes to autumn sun (above). At right, pumpkin carvers concentrate.

ALCHEMIST of autumn has gilded these aspens growing straight and tall (below) in forest near Wilson Mesa, Colorado.

C.D. Dietrich

ECHOES of outdoor concerts linger near this leaf-carpeted New England bandstand.

M.S. Rogers

MAPLE LEAVES form crimson drift (above) against granite wall edging this pasture in Maine.

STOCKPILED WARMTH, neatly stacked and covered, waits in northwestern Minnesota to heat house during upcoming winter.

THE PRIDE IS OBVIOUS in the eyes of this Oklahoma farm boy (right) as he holds part of a golden harvest. And at far right, the bounty of prolific Oregon garden forms colored, multi-textured pile.

Dick Dietrich

Thomas L. Luker

B. March

CINNAMON-HUED trees frame this serene, well-kept farm (right) lying in the hollow of a misty valley of Vermont.

PLUMP PUMPKINS are stacked against this mellow blue barn, ready to become a Halloween prop or a pie.

CONCAVE/CONVEX pattern of mountain and woods—reflected in Maroon Lake in Colorado—provides tranquility for autumn angler.

CRYSTAL RIVER splinters over gravelly Wyoming river bed (far left), as bursts of gold intersperse with the deep hue of evergreens clinging to mountainous backdrop.

UNAWARE and unafraid, white-tail deer stands bathed in autumn sunlight. And, when you turn the page, a rush of water will carry you along as autumn heads out with its last splash of vivid colors.

P. Van Rhijn

L. West

Farewell

"I saw old Autumn in the misty morn, stand shadowless like silence listening."

—Thomas Hood

By Mary Squire
Huntington, New York

Along the Northeast coast, fall comes more slowly than it does inland. In September, the trees are still green, though they have a tired and dusty look, as though summer's heat and humidity have exhausted them. As the school buses start to rumble along rural roads again, the first squadrons of Canada geese begin to return to the ponds from their summer vacations.

The trees are alive with migrating cedar waxwings and a half-dozen different species of warblers. Silent, nervous kinglets flit through the berry-ladened yews. Kingbirds hover like helicopters over the water and dive on choice insects. A flash of blue and his peculiar rattling call heralds the kingfisher on his morning rounds. Hawks and ospreys hunt high over the marsh.

With October comes the morning fog. It is lifting by the time I drive through our village, but it still hovers in the woods, slanting through the trees as the sun emerges. I have to drive slowly down the lane to the harbor to avoid frantic squirrels and chipmunks bringing in their sheaves. So preoccupied are they with their harvest and the necessity of wresting choice bits from greedy neighbors, they pay no attention to such inedible things as cars.

Mist slowly rises from the still ponds where the first few scarlet leaves float motionless. Beautiful, mysterious dragonflies skim the surface of the water. From across the harbor, fish crows scream. No wonder that for centuries the collective noun for them has been a "murder of crows." There is a brief but unmistakable scent of fox along the bank, but I seldom see them—although I did see a weasel one morning.

Blaze of Autumn Color

The beautiful old trees along the village roads are a blaze of New England color by the time the woods along this sheltered harbor begin to turn. Each year I am mystified that one tree will turn overnight, while another of exactly the same species, not 10 feet away, remains green. Difference in soil? Drainage? Early childhood trauma?

The contrasting colors of the vines below the trees make me realize again how far north a jungle can thrive.

Autumn offers a kaleidoscope of colors here along the coast: Red— but still very healthy—poison ivy waves from the top of a black locust. Orange Virginia creeper winds through the dark green yews. Vivid red maples and dogwoods on the edge of the marsh are decorated with the yellow leaves and bright orange berries of bittersweet, while dull yellow wisteria threatens to strangle the Japanese cherry trees at the verge of the marsh. Golden wild grape vines seem to have taken over the entire far side of the big pond.

The colors of autumn know no bounds: Foamy patches of calico asters appear along the road and at the edge of the woods. Lavender and purple New England asters and three kinds of goldenrod join the loosestrife and Joe Pye weed at the ponds' edges.

Harbinger of Days Ahead

The sounds of autumn here along the Northeast coast are a harbinger of days ahead, too. By mid-morning, skeins of honking geese appear overhead. With their wings dipped and landing gear down, they swoop over the marsh and wood and land noisily in the big pond. Another flock lands in the smaller pond farther inland and considerable conversation takes place between the two groups. The second flock takes off again, half of them joining their neighbors on the big pond and the rest circling the marsh.

As yet another boisterous multitude arrives, the need for an air traffic controller becomes evident. As the geese circle the pond—honking for their relatives to get out of the way— they are forced to shear off and try again several times since the water is still full of answering birds.

October's late afternoons have a taste and smell and a color that happens at no other time of the year. My world seems enclosed in an amber light that is almost liquid. An occasional fish jumping is the only motion in our placid harbor. The still water reflects the blazing color of the trees. When the tide is high, it's hard to see where reality stops and illusion begins.

Gulls Follow the Sun

As the tide recedes from the sand bar, the departing laughing gulls mock me as they set off to follow the sun. The great white herons and snowy egrets will be next to leave. The great blue herons will stick around long enough to greet the most charming of all ducks, the buffleheads, for whom the cold, gray harbor is their winter home.

These "rubber-duckies" are nature's compensation for January and

"A FULL HARVEST MOON RISES, TRANSFORMING THE HAZE..."

February, months I could otherwise do without. The herring gulls—bless their greedy hearts—will stay and add their lonely mewling to the winter winds.

By early November, dusk comes too soon. Tree toads, cicadas, crickets and katydids are silenced for another year, but the eerie whistling of the wigeons on the ponds still echoes across the marsh and harbor. As I walk to the car, mist is again rising from the water. Through it, a full harvest moon rises, transforming the haze into an unbelievable pink against the darkening sky.

Then suddenly one night, autumn is swept away. Winter arrives, screaming, on the wings of a nor'easter, shoving white-capped waves into the marsh and ripping away the last clinging leaves.

That's why I make such an effort to enjoy all of autumn's sensory gifts while they last.

Wading

Go wading in the forest
When its floor is golden laid,
And see the splashing autumn leaves
Sailing through the glade.
Look up and see an autumn sky
Above a harvest sea,
Of leaves that fall like colored rain
That patters playfully.

—Hilda Sanderson
Calhoun, Louisiana

M. Roessler

Water wonderland and fisherman's paradise, Michigan has 36,000 miles of rivers, 11,000 inland lakes, and, of course, the Great Lakes. You're never more than 6 miles from water in this state! Rivers such as the Muskegon are ideal for fishing, boating and canoeing—and offer scenic treats, as evidenced by this autumn view of river and colorful trees.

Tunnels To Times Past

COVERED BRIDGES provide links to laid-back days and simpler times.

They have nostalgic appeal that makes you pause and reflect. If you look at these pictures closely and listen carefully, you may hear the clip-clop of hooves and the rumble of wheels, echoes of the days when horse-drawn vehicles traversed each bridge's well-worn planks.

Of over 10,000 covered bridges built across the U.S. between 1805 (after the first was erected in Philadelphia) and the early 20th century, only 893 now remain. Three-quarters of those bridges are found in six states—231 in Pennsylvania, 100 in Vermont, 157 in Ohio, 103 in Indiana, 54 in Oregon and 52 in New Hampshire.

Today, these remaining covered bridges are frequently visited and photographed, as more and more people learn to appreciate these nostalgic pieces of early Americana.

The practical reason for covering bridges was to preserve the wooden span from the forces of nature, which would otherwise reduce a bridge's useful life. In addition, the upright sides of the bridge kept skittish horses from shying at the sight of the water as they crossed.

On the less prosaic side, the roof provided shelter for travelers during rain, welcome shade for young fishermen hanging poles out the side vents and a refuge for courting couples looking for a little privacy.

Photographer Les Kelly of Huntington Beach, California has a fanatic interest in covered bridges, and covered the country to capture this collection of bridges on film. His images are so vivid you can take the same trip from your easy chair, without even fastening your seat belt.

Enjoy.

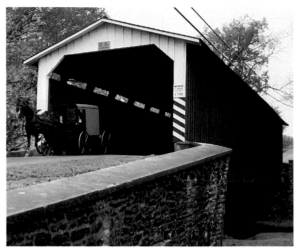

CENTURY-OLD SCENE. An Amish buggy passes through the Leahman Place Bridge in Lancaster County, Pa., as such buggies have rumbled over it for 100 years.

SCENIC SURROUNDINGS. The only historic covered bridge located within a national park, the Wawona spans a river in Yosemite (right). At far right, one of 34 covered bridges in Parke County, Indiana—the Narrows Bridge. The county celebrates its bridges in a 2-week festival in October.

SINCE 1866. For 122 years, the 460-ft. Cornish-Windsor Bridge has spanned the Connecticut River between Cornish, N.H. and Windsor, Vermont. It's the longest remaining covered bridge in the United States. The Warren Bridge, above right, adds a picturesque touch to Warren in central Vermont.

ARCHED OVERHANG enhances the beauty of the rustic Hemlock Bridge, which stands among tall fir trees near Fryeburg, Maine.

CRISS-CROSS. Intersecting boardwork adds extra interest to the Albany Bridge, spanning a rocky river near Passaconaway in the White Mtns. of New Hampshire.

Winter Has Its Own Bewitching Ways

GET OUT the flannel sheets—nature's about to give us its annual cold shoulder. Yet, while winter isn't appreciated by some, it has some "warm", appealing features.

Winter can weave a magical spell, transforming the mundane into the manificent. With each fresh snow, the landscape wears a clean white cloak, hard edges are softened and every color is purified.

When temperatures drop, nature puts up its own decorations—sculpted snow drifts, crystalline icicles, and delicate hoarfrost adding a lacy trim to exposed surfaces.

Winter sets a slower pace, too. It allows time for sitting by a roaring fire to read a book, contemplate, have a family discussion, or just pet the dog.

Our photographers braved some brisk breezes to capture the photos on these pages. But the collective result allows you to experience winter's arrival across the country ...without even leaving the fire.

SNUG SHELTER of Vermont farm buildings (above) shield people and livestock from harsh winter's chill. Left, skier's tracks intersect foot prints in front of Colorado cabin.

CROSS-COUNTRY RUNNER (right) tracks powdered-sugar snow of Penn. clearing.

R. Heinzen

W. Pote: H. Armstrong Roberts

VELVET FILIGREE edges fallen leaves on grassy bed, as winter's fingers tentatively touch the land, getting ready to tuck earth under snowy blanket.

GOLDEN GLOW through windows hints at warmth within the homes in New Hampshire village, welcoming visitors to holiday celebrations.

M. Thonig: H. Armstrong Roberts

George Robinson

Doris Barker

Julie Habel

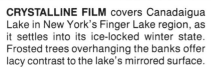

CRYSTALLINE FILM covers Canadaigua Lake in New York's Finger Lake region, as it settles into its ice-locked winter state. Frosted trees overhanging the banks offer lacy contrast to the lake's mirrored surface.

BLIZZARD'S HAZE obscures Iowa fence line (top right) as winter shows its strength. Best part of a day like this is that it promotes one of the season's snowbound pleasures—a good book, warm quilt and soup on the stove.

MERINGUE of freshly fallen snow tops Colorado barn and piles in fluffy heaps on fences. Wonder what's under those mounds?

BARELY FROSTED with snow, rippled landscape forms backdrop for herd of horses being brought down from Wyoming range.

Frank Oberle

WHIPPED CREAM snow forms mounds on river rocks in Sand Harbor area of Lake Tahoe, Nev.

SOLITARY SKIER pauses to enjoy pristine vista of open spaces in Grand Teton National Park.

VERMONT VILLAGE nestles in snow-covered valley, sheltered from whistling wind by rolling hills and sturdy evergreens.

JAGGED GLAZING (left center) coats green wagon, barns, fences and hangs in frozen drops from all vertical surfaces in aftermath of an ice storm near Morristown, New Jersey.

SHADOWED CONTRASTS of tree limbs and new snow weave through Massachusetts scenery, framing snow-wrapped fence and unblemished meadow. And when you turn the page, you'll see a hardworking snowplow against a background of rugged Alaskan mountains, sending up snow in arcing spray as it clears remote, scenic Glenn Highway.

A. Griffin: H. Armstrong Roberts

GLIDING THROUGH A PERFECT WINTER AFTERNOON

THE AIR is crisp and sharp and bites at my nose and cheeks. The sun peeking through spotty clouds gives the hills the illusion of moving light. There is no wind, no sound except for the soft shushing of my skis as I glide over the path on day-old snow.

At first, as always, my arms and legs seem to rebel against the rhythmic push, glide, push, glide, and my breathing is labored. But as I watch the tips of my skis gliding swiftly over the snow-covered trail, my body becomes a part of the movement and a sense of effortlessness comes over me. Now I can relax and look up to enjoy the beauty around me.

The sun dapples the woods with dark shadows and bright glares. Reaching the spot where the trees give way to shrubs and brush at the edge of the meadow, I pause.

Silence Cleanses the Mind

Except for the sound of my breathing, the silence is pure. I stand absolutely still to let it flow around and cleanse my mind. Bathed in quiet, my body warm and relaxed, I seem to be one with creation. My spirit soars and I thank God for the privilege of being alive.

Sparrows, round and warm in their puffed out feathers, seek last year's seeds among the bittersweet draped over a fallen tree. As I move out of the woods and into the meadow, they scatter like so many dry leaves in a wind.

The sky is blue and brilliant now, and it hurts my eyes as I pause to watch a hawk circle and soar, seeking prey.

Here the field is level and smooth. Skiing with practiced ease, I leave a clean trail through the powdery new snow. I shush up a steep hill, then hesitate at the top, anticipating the rush of the long drop. As I begin the descent, the snow is smooth and slick and I quickly pick up speed. The sensation of flying is mingled with a fear of falling, and I reach the bottom with a sense of accomplishment.

The trail turns toward home now, following the edge of the cornfield. Not all the corn was harvested last fall and rows of stalks still stand at attention. Crows feeding here scold me as I pass by. I picture how, toward evening, the deer will come out of the pines, walking carefully through the deep snow on their small hooves to feed right here on the leftover ears.

A Perfect Winter Afternoon

I'm tiring now. One last hill to climb, then a detour around our small pond nestled like a jewel in a ring of ice-bound cattails. I notice vapor rising in fairy-tale wisps from the small stream that feeds this pond. There is a profound peace in this place, and I soak it up on this *perfect* winter afternoon.

Finally, I conclude I have rested too long—the cold is beginning to creep into my hands and feet. Turning my back on the pond, I head for home, sliding my skis with detectibly less energy than before.

I can see the house over the rise now, with its rows of firewood neatly stacked outside the back door and smoke comfortably curling from the chimney. It's "home", and it beckons me with its warmth. I approach eagerly, ready to resume my responsibilities. I have been renewed.

By Margaret A. Villanova, Manlius, New York

Kurt Thorsen

A Flock of Good Reasons To Keep a Few Chickens

*By Peggy Beals
Marshfield, Massachusetts*

"WHY DO YOU keep chickens?" young visitors often ask. "Don't you have enough money to buy eggs?"

Some freezing mornings and stormy nights—as I brave the elements to tend my little charges—I wonder the same thing. But not for long.

I could cite economy. These hens and their arrogant escort—the proud rooster—replace several energy-gulping appliances.

They are also great garbage disposals. I promote so much free food for them that a bag of "Beals' peels" is a standard feature among our friends. They drop off apple peels, potato peels and other scraps as they drive by our place.

They are shredder grinders. People come from afar to dump their leaf rakings into our chicken yard. I stuff more into their house for litter. We throw them pulled weeds and prunings. They work it all over constantly, creating a fine mulch.

I could cite productivity. They lay gourmet-sized eggs, thick whites cupped around deep orange meaty yolks. And I *know* they're fresh.

"Eggs," the old timers used to say, "are a nice by-product." Those seasoned farmers contended the real worth of hens is the fertilizer they provide. There's plenty of that, and lots of muscle-stretching exercise in shifting it from the pen to the garden!

I could even sermonize on the satisfaction of moving toward a self-sustaining homestead—the house, hens and garden working together to produce food and utilize wastes.

Need To Be Needed

But there's more than those hard-headed reasons to keeping hens. Some of us "empty nesters" have trouble adjusting after the children have left. We don't feel *needed* when household demands slack off.

Hens are easier to care for than children, but they do keep you up, out and doing. It's energizing to breathe crisp, clean air at 7 a.m., and satisfying to watch the birds busying themselves about breakfast, pecking into their pan of hot, flavored mash.

After a busy day, it's an interlude of tranquility to go close them in, then stand alone in the hush of the chicken yard, watching sunset tint the willows coral, or a distant plane arc the starry sky.

And there's always the daily surprise: How many eggs will I gather today in my treasured egg basket? (That basket was a gift of a young friend who enjoys our "cackleberries".)

Without the hens, I'd certainly miss the simple pleasure of sitting next to their yard, sipping a cup of tea and watching them peck and scratch, stretch their wings lazily in the sun, or stand regarding me quizzically, eager for some sort of action.

Who needs aerobics, gadgets, or pale watery eggs when a little home flock of useful "girls" is so rewarding?

It's for those reasons, young friends, I still keep a few chickens.

Yosemite's splendor is awe-inspiring—from El Capitan's sheer face to 3,000-ft. Glacier Point to the 8,852-ft. elevation of Half-Dome, with Bridal Veil Falls leaping free in the foreground. This glacier-carved canyon's waterfalls, towering cliffs, rounded domes and massive monoliths have long fascinated visiting artists and photographers.

Winter Noise

Silently they fall—the first snowflakes,
  shrouding the world in white.
Cold and wondrous—this winter season
  icy streams bubbling over stones
  chickadees and finches
  calling to their mates.
Through woods of bare treetops
  old man winter whispers his frosty breath
  branches creak and sway in the frozen silence,
  echoes of woodpeckers tap, tap, tapping.
A pause and then—
  the thunderous quiet of winter.

—Sandra Barnosky, Brunswick, Ohio

My Thankful List

By Jan Roat, Red Lodge, Montana

AT THANKSGIVING, like most people, my "thankful list" used to include family, friends, health, shelter, living in the U.S....all the usual.

But, during the winter's short days and long nights here in south central Montana, I have a lot of time to think. So I've come to realize that my personal list of things to be thankful for includes items that likely deviate somewhat from the norm.

Therefore, at Thanksgiving, I'm especially thankful for:

...whoever invented 4-wheel-drive and the snowmobile; when snow drifts over our fences we still must get off the ranch for food and supplies.

...the gentle drift of large snowflakes playing tag in the breeze.

...a Chinook wind in January that eats away the snow.

...the lilting song of chickadees who find something to be cheerful about even when it's below zero.

...a crackling fire on a frigid day, a new book and the time to read it.

...a roomful of rainbows reflecting from frosted crystals in the windows.

...the pure white of sparkling fresh snow on a sun-brightened day.

...the warmth of geraniums blooming on my side of the window while snow piles up a pane away.

...the swish of skis through powdery snow accompanied by the exhilarating rush of clean, crisp air.

...our ever-changing, all-enduring Montana mountains, lifting our eyes and soul toward the heavens.

...the first bits of sky-blue and sun-yellow as crocus peek through February snow banks, making a welcome sight after months of an all-white world.

These are just a few of the things about winter that bring joy to my heart...and make my own personal Thanksgiving last longer than a day.

M. Thonig/H.Armstrong Roberts

Warm Look at Winter

SOME people are just born with talent. Julie Habel, an Iowa farm wife, is one of those people.

She has no formal training in photography, yet she has a knack for knowing what makes a good picture. She continually sends us "irresistible" pictures for *Country* and our company's other three magazines.

Here's photo evidence. We feel she's captured the essence of winter in rural America, from the warm feeling you get while viewing the photo of the farmer and young daughter bringing in the eggs...to a pair of jeans caught in an unexpected snow while drying on the line...to the tender touch of the rugged farmer above who stuffed that contented piglet in his bib overalls!

These pictures need no captions. Julie's camera lens tells it all.

Spend more time in the country with our "family" of country-oriented magazines!

If you like this book, you'll *love* the four magazines published by the same firm—Reiman Publications. Each magazine brings you a bit of the country all year 'round! Here's a brief description of them:

Country is the magazine "for those who live in or long for the country." More than 700,000 people have subscribed after seeing just one sample issue!

They enjoy its beautiful photographs, ad-free format and fascinating features about people who love country life. It offers something for every member of the family...a Country Decorating Section ...Crafts and Food Sections...a Country Kids Section...essays and articles about country life...poetry ..."tours" of country properties, inns and bed 'n breakfasts...and color photos of country scenes so vibrant you'll want to cut them out and frame them!

Whether you are living in the country or longing for it, you will love *Country* magazine!

Country Woman is the only national magazine *exclusively* for women who enjoy country living.

Most of each issue is written by readers, as they exchange light-hearted ideas and anecdotes, country recipes, decorating ideas, crafts and even nostalgic photos.

Each issue features photo tour of one of the best kitchens in the country...plus elaborate food section displays recipes in convenient "recipe card cut-out" format. Over 400,000 loyal subscribers love this "warm" magazine!

Country Handcrafts brings 30 fresh, original projects in each bimonthly, book-sized issue. There is *no advertising* in this magazine. Instead, it's filled cover-to-cover with handcrafts. Each project is pictured in full color photos that show every detail, and the FULL-SIZED pat-

tern for every project is provided *right in the issue*—there are no additional patterns to order, and no need for time-consuming enlarging.

Country Handcrafts is the crafts magazine more than 600,000 subscribers look forward to receiving six times a year. They enjoy a variety of craft techniques—knit, crochet, wood-working and painting, basket-weaving, jewelry-making, applique, quilting, and more!

Farm & Ranch Living isn't just for farmers! Anyone who grew up in the country or who's curious about farm and ranch life will love "visiting" over 70 farms and ranches a year, without leaving the easy chair!

Each issue features four day-by-day, full-month diaries kept by farm and ranch families in different parts of the country, describing in detail their life in rural America. In addition, there's a photo tour of a beautiful farm or ranch in each issue, including a "walk" through the house.

Readers regularly meet America's "Most Interesting" farmers and ranchers...reminisce about the "good old days" on the farm...and sit down to eat in farmers' favorite cafes! Get a firsthand "feel" for farm and ranch life through the pages of *Farm & Ranch Living!*

TO ORDER a copy of this *A Year in the Country* book (at $17.98 plus $3.00 postage/handling), or to order any of the four magazines described here (sample copy $2.98 each; 1 year subscription $14.98 each), use one of the order cards at right. Or charge your order by calling toll-free 1-800/558-1013. (In Wis., dial 1-800/242-6065.)